Creating
NIM
GAMES

Math Projects Series
Sherron Pfeiffer

Dale Seymour Publications®

Project Editor: Joan Gideon

Production Coordinator: Shannon Miller

Art: Rachel Gage and Joe Conte

Text Design: Polly Christensen

Cover Design: Polly Christensen

m&m's® is a registered trademark of Mars Candy, Inc.

Many of the designations used by manufacturers and sellers to distinguish their products are claimed as trademarks. Where those designations appear in this book and Addison Wesley Longman was aware of a trademark claim, the designations have been printed with initial capital letters.

Published by Dale Seymour Publications®, an imprint of Addison Wesley Longman Inc.

Order Number DS21844

ISBN 1-57232-272-1

1 2 3 4 5 6 7 8 9 10-VG-01 00 99 98 97

This product is printed on recycled paper

Contents

Teaching with NIM 1

What Is NIM? 1
Mathematics Objectives Addressed by NIM 1
NIM as a Worthwhile Task 3
Introducing a NIM Game 3
Creating New NIM Games 6
Assessing Student Learning 7
    Student Checklist 9
    Sprouts 10

Section 1—NIM Games 13

Stuff NIM 14
Classic NIM 16
Array NIM 18
Calculator NIM 22
Pattern Block NIM 24
Add-Up NIM 28
Triangular NIM 33
Integer NIM 37
Path NIM 39

Section 2—Student Project 41

Project Introduction 43
Student Sheet 1—Project Overview 47
Student Sheet 2—Reminder Page 48
Student Sheet 3—Title and Theme 49
Student Sheet 4—Game Rules 50
Student Sheet 5—Playing Board and Pieces 51
Student Sheet 6—Finishing and Packaging 52
Student Sheet 7—Oral Presentation 53
Student Sheet 8—Evaluation 54
Sample Student Projects and Evaluations 55

Teaching with NIM

Oh, I know – NIM is a Notorious Illusive Mammal!

What Is NIM?

Many people believe the Chinese invented the game of NIM many centuries ago. Others have suggested it may be a variation of the ancient African game Mancala, which involves placing pebbles in pits and removing them according to certain rules. Regardless of its origin, NIM is one of the oldest mathematical strategy games, and it has remained popular through the centuries. At the turn of the century, Charles Bouton, a Harvard professor, gave this group of games its name—NIM. *Nim* is a verb form meaning "to take."

There are many NIM games. The rules are simple; but finding a winning strategy is quite challenging. To play NIM, arrange a certain number of objects in some specified way, or establish a target number. Each player takes a turn removing, or adding, up to a specific number of objects. The player taking the last object or reaching the established target either wins or loses, depending upon how winning is defined. Part of NIM's intrigue must certainly be due to its simplicity; it can be learned easily in a few minutes. However, it can take days, even a lifetime, to master. NIM is not a game of chance; no dice nor spinners are used.

Perhaps the most popular form of NIM involves arranging objects in rows and allowing players to remove as many objects on their turn as they want, provided the objects are all from the same row. The winner takes the last object(s). This version is sometimes called Classic NIM. Many machines have been designed and built to play this version of NIM. In 1940, Edward Condon invented the Nimatron, a one-ton machine that played games with four rows of up to seven counters each. It was displayed at the New York World's Fair and won nearly every game it played. (*Problem-Solving with NIM*, No. A-257. MECC, Minneapolis, Minn., p. 1.)

Mathematics Objectives Addressed by NIM

"Problem solving should be the central focus of the mathematics curriculum. As such, it is a primary goal of all mathematics instruction and an integral part of all mathematical activity. Problem solving is not a distinct topic but a process that should

Rules of Classic NIM

1. Arrange the markers in three rows with 3 in one row, 5 in a second row, and 7 in the third row.

   • • •

   • • • • •

   • • • • • • •

2. Take turns taking as many as you want but only from one row. You can take an entire row if you want.
3. No skipping turns.
4. The winner takes the last one.

Teaching Strategies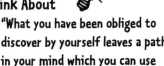

One of the greatest challenges for teachers who engage their students in problem solving is deciding when to assist and when to wait. When a student is feeling frustration, it is difficult to avoid stepping in. After all, we don't want the student to give up! Yet, we also don't want to deprive the student of the great joy experienced when solving a challenging problem. More often than not, students will persist and resolve problems if the teacher resists the urge to step in with too much help.

Think About

"What you have been obliged to discover by yourself leaves a path in your mind which you can use again when the need arises."
—G. C. Lichtenburg

"Are your students puzzled and moderately frustrated? Good! This is a sign that learning is going on."
—Thomas C. O'Brien

Or perhaps NIM means Natali Is Moving

permeate the entire program and provide the context in which concepts and skill can be learned." *Curriculum and Evaluation Standards for School Mathematics* (Reston, Va.: National Council of Teachers of Mathematics, 1989, p. 23.) Research and effective classroom practice have shown that the most effective approach is to infuse problem solving and thinking skills into the content areas. If NIM is included in the area of mathematics, which objectives and goals are being addressed?

Numeration. NIM players use physical materials to develop number concepts; use a variety of counting strategies; recognize multiple uses of numbers; and develop and apply number theory concepts relating to primes, factors, and multiples.

Classification, Pattern, and Seriation. NIM players describe groupings and patterns; extend and create patterns in a variety of forms while describing the pattern's properties; order events by logical reasoning; use patterns to make predictions and solve problems; use patterns to identify relationships within the number system; and model the concept of a variable.

Problem Solving. NIM players communicate mathematical ideas by explaining processes, results, and personal problem-solving strategies; demonstrate a variety of ways to solve problems using spatial sense and visual memory; evaluate solutions to problems; verify and interpret results with respect to the original situation; develop an organized approach to solving routine and nonroutine problems; use problem-solving methods to investigate mathematical content and to formulate problems; use reasoning as well as other ways to validate thinking and recognize various points of view; make and evaluate conjectures and arguments; use deductive and inductive reasoning; and demonstrate creativity, confidence, and competence in using mathematics.

Data Collection, Display, and Interpretation. NIM players collect, organize, and explain data gathered through a variety of experiments; and they formulate and solve problems that involve collecting, displaying, and interpreting data.

Computation. NIM players demonstrate the meaning of addition and subtraction through models and solve problems using basic operations with numbers.

Obviously, NIM games can help you accomplish many of the objectives from the mathematics curriculum!

NIM as a Worthwhile Task

When designing the learning environment, select worthwhile tasks that create opportunities for students to develop their mathematical understandings, competencies, and interests. These tasks should do the following:

- include sound and significant mathematics
- take into account students' understandings, interests, and experiences
- take into account the diverse ways students learn
- engage students' intellects and encourage "what if" questions
- call for problem forming, problem solving, and decision making
- promote communication about math
- nest skill development in the context of problem solving
- be accessible to all students at the start, but challenging to those with high levels of understanding
- stimulate students to make connections (math strand to math strand and math to other curricula)
- engage or be enjoyable for the majority of students

Does NIM fit the above descriptions? Absolutely! NIM also uses simple materials such as coins, sticks, and other easy-to-find objects. Especially impressive is the fact that NIM is accessible to even preschoolers while challenging the most sophisticated of mathematical minds! For all of these reasons, this author considers NIM a perfect activity.

Essence of NIM

NIM is a perfect activity!

- It addresses a great many of the objectives in the math curriculum.
- It offers extensive opportunity for nonroutine problem solving.
- It is accessible to everyone at the start.
- It is extendible and challenging to even the most sophisticated.
- It requires easy-to-obtain and simple materials.
- It can be introduced and explored in short periods of time.

Introducing a NIM Game

Although you may begin with any NIM game, a good first NIM game, because of its simplicity and relationship to number, is Balloon Ride NIM (from Jean K. Stenmark, et al. *Family Math.* Berkeley, California: Equals, Lawrence Hall of Science, 1986. pp. 30–31).

Begin by telling this story: "A fair is in town, and one of the rides is a hot air balloon. However, tickets aren't for sale. The only way to ride on the hot air balloon is to win this game. The balloon is anchored to the ground with ten ropes. We will take turns cutting one or two ropes. The last person to cut a rope (or ropes) wins the ride."

Using a model of some kind, play the game with you as one player and the class as the second player. The model might be a picture of a balloon on a poster with ten pieces of heavy yarn hanging down, or a balloon filled with helium and ten pieces of curly ribbon tied to the bottom. (Tie a bell or some other weight to the ribbons so the balloon will stay anchored to the floor until you

Teaching Strategies

Can a teacher pose a problem without knowing the solution? Absolutely!

If problem solving is what we do when we don't know what to do, how do we model problem solving if we always have the answers? With the courage and self-confidence to solve a problem in front of students, teachers can present a powerful model of how to approach problems. Teachers can demonstrate how to get started, persist, try alternative strategies, and enjoy the process.

Teaching Strategies

You can learn a great deal about how students go about solving problems by observing them as they play NIM games.

- Do they play with no attention to what is happening other than "I won"?
- Do they repeat moves that don't relate to winning strategies?
- Do they keep track of what is happening?
- Do they look for ways to record data?
- Do they use these data to help devise strategies or theories?
- Do they try a variety of theories?
- Do they try variations such as making a smaller version, working backward, and looking for patterns?
- Do they consider all the options rather than jumping to quick answers based on limited effort or information?

cut the last piece.) The model could be as simple as a picture of a hot-air balloon, such as the one in *Family Math,* and ten toothpicks on an overhead projector.

Ask students if they want to go first or second by having them hold up one or two fingers in a vote. Go with the most popular choice.

Proceed by taking turns, you take one or two ropes on your turn and the class takes one or two (again voting by holding up one or two fingers). While playing, ask the class to report how many ropes are left after each turn. Also ask questions such as, "Is that an odd or even number?" When the game has ended, ask the class whether the first or second player won the game.

Emphasize that the goal in playing this game is to find a winning strategy. Can you win by always going first? Second? Does it matter? Are there any strategic moves? Encourage students to keep track of what is happening as they play.

Direct students to work in pairs playing the game and searching for winning strategies. Give each pair ten objects (such as ice-cream sticks, cubes, or Cuisenaire® rods) to represent balloon anchors. Tell students they are expected to be in charge of the materials, and ask them to explain what that means. When students set their own guideline for appropriate behavior they are more likely to be responsible.

While students play, circulate among groups and check to make sure everyone understands the rules. Watch for emerging theories. Encourage students to develop theories instead of focusing on just the number of times they or their opponents have won. Ask them to think about how to collect the game data such as, whether the first or second player is winning.

After about ten minutes, stop the class and ask everyone to cover their materials and focus up front. Have students explain their strategies. You might even want to write them on the board. Some students will not have strategies yet. Have students play again and try one of the strategies on the board.

Allow more playing time. Then refocus the class and suggest these strategies.

- Make a smaller version of the problem. Start with a game that has three ropes.
- Work backward. Continue adding ropes until the game reaches ten.
- Make a table and look for a pattern.

Number of Markers	To Win
3	be second
4	be first, take 1
5	be first, take 2
6	be second, leave 3

Ask students to go home and play this game with someone. Have them write about what happened and their strategies.

The next day, ask students to share their strategies again. A few students might be invited to play at the overhead to model their strategies. Have other students reflect upon these strategies and express their thoughts about each.

These are examples of student strategies for Balloon Ride NIM.
- "I play until we get down to six left and then I begin to think."
- "I take the opposite of what my partner takes. If she takes one, I take two, and if she takes two, I take one."
- "I try to leave my partner with an odd number."
- "I always want to go first."
- "I think it has something to do with multiples."

Now that your students know how to play a NIM game, present a new NIM game every two to three days over the next few weeks. Make copies of the game sheets in Section 1 to hand out to students. Each game sheet is followed by a sheet that suggests new games and things to think about in discovering a strategy. These sheets can be filled out by your students and kept in their math portfolio.

Follow this process each time you present a game.
1. Explain the game rules.
2. Play the game with the class for about ten minutes (you are one player, the class is the other).
3. Have students play in pairs in class and at home to search for winning strategies. Have them record their strategies under the Your Own Strategies section of the strategy sheets.
4. On subsequent days, ask students to share their strategies with the entire class.
5. Have pairs of students test various strategies.
6. Discuss extensions or ways to vary the rules to create a new game. Give students time to try their ideas for changing a rule or two in each game. Have them write their ideas under the Your Own Games sections of the game sheets. This will prepare them for creating their own games in Section 2.

Your students will begin to come up with lots of strategies. Here are some students have given.

For Array NIM (page 18)
"I capture the corners."
"I try to leave holes for final plays."
"It's like tic-tac-toe, take control by playing in the middle."
"I mirror what my partner does."

... or ... Notify Iris Monday

MEMO

NIM Contest
How about a contest to come up with clever answers to, "What could NIM stand for?"
For example,
    Nifty in Math
    Ninety Incorporated Moms
    Noses in Motion
    NIM Improves Minds

Essence of NIM

NIM Variables

- total number of target numbers
- the number taken or placed on a turn
- the definition of winning
- spatial placement and rules
- themes

For Pattern Block NIM (page 24)

"I play the triangles to leave more chances to play."

"We work backward with this game by placing six triangles on the hexagon and removing them one at a time to figure out whether to go first or second."

"Leave holes."

"I play the same piece my partner plays."

"Go second."

Creating New NIM Games

After students have experience playing a NIM game, ask, "What variables can you change to make a new NIM game?"

By changing the variables in NIM, students can create an infinite number of new games. Consider this list of variables.

- Vary the number used in the game. Instead of 10 ropes, why not 19 or 13? With calculators instead of objects, students could use larger numbers, such as 100.
- Vary the number taken or placed on a turn. Instead of one or two, how about up to three or nine?
- Vary the definition of winning. Instead of winning by taking or placing the last marker, win by forcing your opponent to place or take the last marker. Or the winner is the one player holding an even number (or odd number) of objects at the end of the game.
- Add a rule about spatial placement of objects. Consider Classic NIM, where objects taken must be in the same row. The rule might state that if two ropes are cut in Balloon Ride NIM, they must be adjacent to each other.
- Reverse play up to a point. While playing Balloon Ride, you could choose to return the ropes you have taken. You will continue to return ropes until you run out of ropes or decide to start taking ropes again. This reversing process could only be done once during a game.
- Use a different theme. *The North Carolina Grades One and Two Assessment, Mathematics* (Raleigh, N. C.: North Carolina Department of Public Instruction, Publications, 1989) has a Balloon Ride variation called Apple Alley. The playing board is a line of apple shapes. The markers could be small toy apples.

In Section 2, students create their own NIM games. They develop themes, rules, playing boards, and packaging for their games. As adults, we are always evaluated based upon the quality of the products we create. Students need opportunities to work over a period of time to create quality products. With the coaching approach that provides feedback presented in Section 2, students will have an opportunity to produce quality work.

Assessing Student Learning

Assessment should produce a biography of a student's learning. It helps you understand what meanings students assign to the ideas being covered. Teachers have always used their own informed professional judgment to evaluate student progress and understanding. This judgment needs to be trusted and validated. More than test scores needs to be communicated about a student's strengths, thinking processes, and needs. You are the best resource for providing this wealth of information! Because of their non-routine nature, NIM games offer opportunities to document a variety of student understandings and behaviors.

First, establish a list of desired problem-solving behaviors. You could involve the class in a brainstorming session to answer the question, "How might you describe a good problem solver?" For example, a problem solver is

- persistent (sticks with a problem)
- confident (makes positive statements about own and others' abilities)
- competent (successful)
- cooperative (works well with others)
- a communicator (explains ideas and processes clearly)
- flexible (willing to try many different strategies and ideas)
- supportive (encourages others to participate and contribute)
- a listener (tries to understand others' ideas and gives positive feedback)
- patient (gathers all the facts first and restrains from jumping to conclusions)
- thorough (considers alternatives and other possible answers)
- enthusiastic (enjoys working on problems and finding new ones)

Student Checklist. The Student Checklist on page 9 lists these problem-solving behaviors. Use this checklist while observing a group of students at work. Plan to observe a different group each day until you have documented the behavior of every student in class. If you have five or six students in a group, add more name columns to the checklist. You can assign a code to indicate the extent to which you observe each behavior for each student. This code might be M = most of the time, S = some of the time, and N = not yet. Or you can document these behaviors by writing anecdotal notes on the checklist that indicate how the student demonstrated the behavior. For example, "Rebecca asked her partner, 'What do you think about the idea of always going first?'" This might be recorded next to *supportive* on the checklist.

Teaching Strategies

When using the Student Checklist, write notes for one group on one paper. Then make 3 copies. Delete the names of students 2, 3, and 4 from one sheet. This becomes the copy that goes into student 1's portfolio. On a second copy, delete the names of students 1, 3, and 4. This copy goes into student 2's portfolio, and so on. This way you avoid rewriting notes and have a record that shows how a given student was functioning in comparison to others in the group.

Teaching Strategies

The act of teaching should be founded upon dialogues between teachers and students. Assessment refers to the process of trying to understand what meanings students assign to the ideas being covered in these dialogues.

Think About

"Teaching is effective to the extent that it takes students thinking into consideration."

NCTM *Curriculum and Evaluation Standards for School Mathematics*, p. 203.

Think About

Is tic-tac-toe a game of NIM? If yes, why? If no, how might it be varied in order to become a game of NIM?

Think About

Keep in mind whoever explains and elaborates is the one who learns! It seems that in many classrooms, it is the teacher doing the learning.

Another approach to using the list of behaviors might be to focus on a few behaviors at a time. Announce to the class the behaviors you're looking for. Students will exaggerate practicing these behaviors at first, which is fine because this is how new behaviors begin. As you circulate, carry a clipboard with large peel-off labels and a pen. When you see a student practicing a behavior, write the student's name and the behavior on a label. At the end of the day, stick the labels in the students' folders or portfolios.

Written Assignments. Ask students to explain and write about their thinking. If it is hard to find time to write during the school day, use the strategy sheet as a homework assignment. For example, ask students to write about their strategies for winning a particular NIM game. Evaluate these papers using a holistic approach. This involves judging student work based on overall impressions rather than small bits of knowledge. This method encourages looking for students' thinking and minimizes the need for structuring questions to elicit predetermined answers. While judging a piece as a whole, ask questions such as, Does it contain some outstanding feature? Does it show a spark of originality? Has the problem been extended? Is the presentation coherent? Sort the papers into three groups: those with something special or impressive, those that meet basic expectations, and those that need reworking. It is important to keep in mind that some students, especially young ones, may understand much more than they communicate through explanations, written or oral. Therefore, always combine teacher observation with student products to create a complete picture of student understanding.

The Sprouts Game. Another way to assess students is to introduce a new strategy game and ask whether or not it is a NIM game. Then ask students to justify their thinking. The Sprouts game on page 10 is an interesting game to use for this kind of analysis. After partners play the game, they can answer the Sprouts Questions for Partners page 11 and the Sprouts Individual Assessment questions on page 12. This assessment helps you learn more about what sense students are making of the essence of NIM. Before creating their own NIM games, students need to understand what is and is not part of NIM. For example, chance is not part of NIM, while making decisions related to a playing strategy is part of NIM.

Student Checklist

Date _____ Action Observed	Student 1 _____	Student 2 _____	Student 3 _____	Student 4 _____
Persistent (sticks with a problem)				
Confident (makes positive statements)				
Competent (successful)				
Cooperative (works well with others)				
A communicator (explains ideas and processes clearly)				
Flexible (willing to try many different strategies and ideas)				
Supportive (encourages others to participate and contribute)				
A listener (tries to under-stand others' ideas and gives positive feedback)				
Patient (gathers all the facts first and restrains from jumping to conclusions)				
Thorough (considers alterna-tives and other possible answers)				
Enthusiastic (enjoys working on problems and finding new ones)				

Sprouts Game

Sprouts is a topological network game. Or, in plain English, it is a game of drawing points and lines.

Start with 2 points, and take turns drawing lines by these rules.

1. A line must start and end at a point. (Curved lines are okay, and you may draw a loop and end at the same point where you started.)

2. After you draw a line, you must mark a new point somewhere on it.

3. No line can cross itself or another line or pass through any point.

You can't draw this line. It crosses another line.

4. No point can have more than 3 lines coming from it.

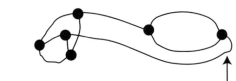

This point has 4 lines coming from it.

5. The winner is the last person able to play.

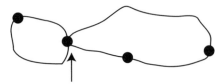

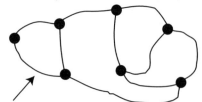

The winner drew this.

© Dale Seymour Publications®

Sprouts Questions for Partners

Play Sprouts with a partner, and then answer these questions.

1. What is the maximum number of moves possible in this game? Explain your answer and draw an example. (15 points)

2. What is the minimum number of moves possible? Explain your answer and draw an example. (15 points)

3. Decide whether or not this is a type of NIM game and support your position. (15 points)

Total Points for Partners _____

Sprouts Individual Assessment

1. Explain your theories about how to always win a Sprouts NIM game. (25 points)

2. Change your theories about how to always win a Sprouts NIM game. (25 points)

2. Change 1 rule of the Sprouts NIM game. Write this changed rule and explain how this changes your thinking about how to win at Sprouts NIM. (30 points)

Total Points for Partners _____

Individual Points _____

Total _____

© Dale Seymour Publications®

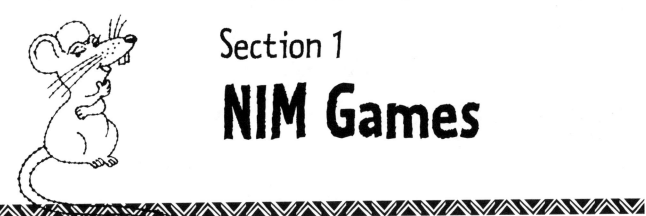

Section 1
NIM Games

Stuff NIM   14

Classic NIM   16

Array NIM   18

Calculator NIM   22

Pattern Block NIM   24

Add Up NIM   28

Triangular NIM   33

Integer NIM   37

Path NIM   39

Stuff NIM

Materials

- a collection of markers such as coins, toothpicks, plastic chips, or buttons

How to Play

1. Decide upon a number of markers to play with. For example, you might start with 14 markers.
2. Lay out this collection in a line.
3. Take turns picking up 1 or 2 markers at a time.
4. No skipping turns.
5. The winner takes the last 1 or 2.

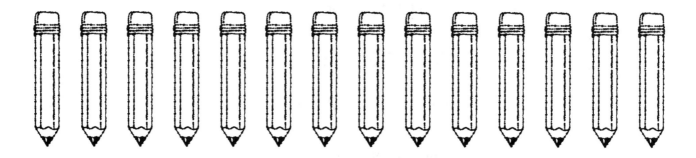

Stuff NIM Strategy

Strategy Ideas

Can you find some patterns related to the total number of markers and the greatest number that can be taken on a turn? Do you want to go first? Should you leave your opponent with an odd number or an even number of markers at the end of your turn?

Your Own Strategies

New Game Ideas

- Change the number of markers in the collection.
- Change the number that can be taken on a turn.
- Require players to take adjacent markers if they take more than 1.
- Allow players to reverse the direction of play. A player can decide they will replace what they've taken (1 or 2 at a time) until the other player decides to start taking again or runs out of markers. A player can only reverse direction once during the game.
- Win by having an even number of markers at the end of the game.

Your Own Games

Classic NIM

© Dale Seymour Publications®

Materials

- 15 of any kind of marker such as coins, plastic chips, buttons, or blocks

How to Play

1. Arrange the markers in three rows with 3 in one row, 5 in a second row, and 7 in the third row.
2. Take turns taking as many as you want but only from one row. You can take an entire row if you want.
3. No skipping turns.
4. The winner forces the other person to take the last one.

Arrange the markers like this.

Classic NIM Strategy

Strategy Ideas

What is the simplest version of this game? How about playing with rows of 1, 3, and 5? Do you see any patterns? Are there any patterns related to even and odd numbers in rows or even and odd numbers of rows?

Your Own Strategies

New Game Ideas

- Change the number of rows.
- Change the numbers in each row.
- To win, take the last marker or markers.

Your Own Games

Array NIM

How to Play

1. Take turns placing a marker in 1 or 2 squares at a time.
2. If 2 markers are placed on a turn, they must be in squares that share a complete side. (They do not need to be next to other squares that contain markers.)

Placing 2 markers on a turn:

These are allowed.   This is not allowed.

3. No skipping turns.
4. The winner places the last 1 or 2 markers.

© Dale Seymour Publications®

Array NIM Strategy

Strategy Ideas

Use a smaller playing board such as 2 squares by 3 squares. Play with the same rules and look for patterns.

   After testing other playing boards, look for general rules to describe winning strategies for groups of boards. Is there a strategy for boards with even numbers of squares per side? What about those with odd numbers per side? Do these dimensions have anything to do with a strategy? Or, is the total number of the squares more important?

Your Own Strategies

New Game Ideas

- Change the shape of the playing board. How about a 4-by-5 array? How about a board that isn't a rectangular array?
- Change the number of markers you can place per turn. How about placing up to 3 markers, keeping the rule that they must be in squares that share complete sides?
- To win, force your opponent to place the last marker.

Your Own Games

More Array NIM Playing Boards

Create Your Own Array
NIM Board

<table>
<tr><td></td><td></td><td></td><td></td><td></td><td></td></tr>
<tr><td></td><td></td><td></td><td></td><td></td><td></td></tr>
<tr><td></td><td></td><td></td><td></td><td></td><td></td></tr>
<tr><td></td><td></td><td></td><td></td><td></td><td></td></tr>
<tr><td></td><td></td><td></td><td></td><td></td><td></td></tr>
<tr><td></td><td></td><td></td><td></td><td></td><td></td></tr>
<tr><td></td><td></td><td></td><td></td><td></td><td></td></tr>
<tr><td></td><td></td><td></td><td></td><td></td><td></td></tr>
</table>

Calculator NIM

Materials

- a calculator

How to Play

1. Choose a target number, such as 21.
2. Enter the target number into the calculator.
3. Take turns subtracting 1, 2, or 3 on a turn. For example, to subtract 2, press [–] [2] then [=].
4. No skipping turns.
5. The winner subtracts the last number to make the calculator display 0.

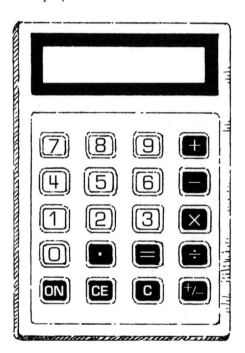

Calculator NIM Strategy

Strategy Ideas

If you can only take up to 3 on a turn, what number do you want to leave your opponent to ensure a win? Is there any connection between the number that can be subtracted on a turn and the target number?

Your Own Strategies

New Game Ideas

- Change the target number.
- Add to get to the target instead of subtracting from the target to get to 0.
- Change the number that can be subtracted on a turn.
- To win, force your opponent to subtract the last number.

Your Own Games

Pattern Block NIM

© Dale Seymour Publications®

Materials

- pattern block shapes—red trapezoids, blue rhombi, and green triangles
- playing board or yellow hexagons

How to Play

1. Take turns placing a trapezoid, rhombus, or triangle on the board (or on a hexagon).
2. Blocks must be placed so that at least one side lines up with one side of the board.

   Place blocks like this.

   Do not place them like this.

3. No skipping turns.
4. The winner places the last block.
5. Allow placing blocks across black lines when the playing board is larger. Here's a trapezoid placed across the center line of a double hexigon board.

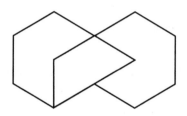

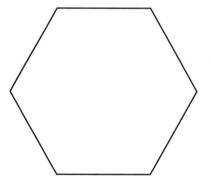

Pattern Block NIM Strategy

Strategy Ideas

Why wouldn't you want to place a trapezoid first? When would you want to place the trapezoid second?

What are all the different ways to cover a yellow hexagon with the red trapezoids, blue rhombi, and green triangles? Does knowing this help find a strategy?

If the triangle is defined as 1 unit of area, what is the area of the hexagon, trapezoid, and blue rhombus? Does this help you find a strategy? Is there some relationship between the total area of any playing board and the winning strategy?

Think about what happens when new pieces are placed on the board in such a way as to leave holes between blocks.

Your Own Strategies

New Game Ideas

- Change the playing board by adding on more hexagons.
- What if you win by forcing the other person to place the last block?

Your Own Games

More Pattern Block NIM Playing Boards

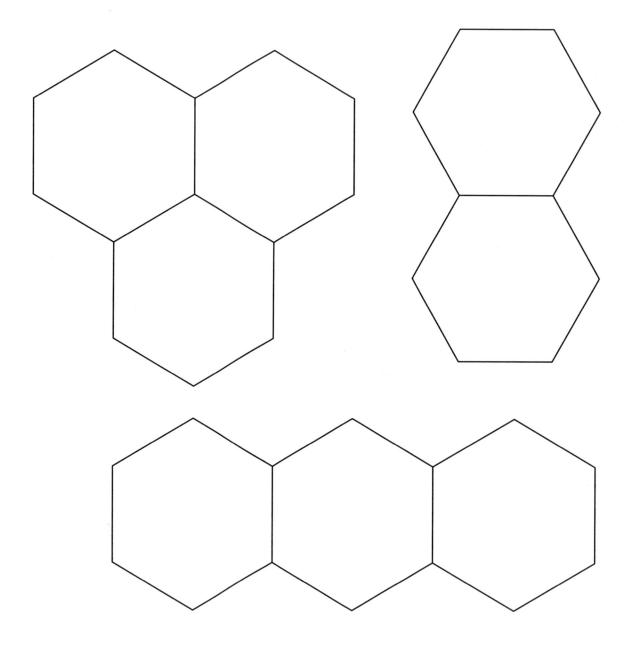

Create Your Own Pattern
Block NIM Board

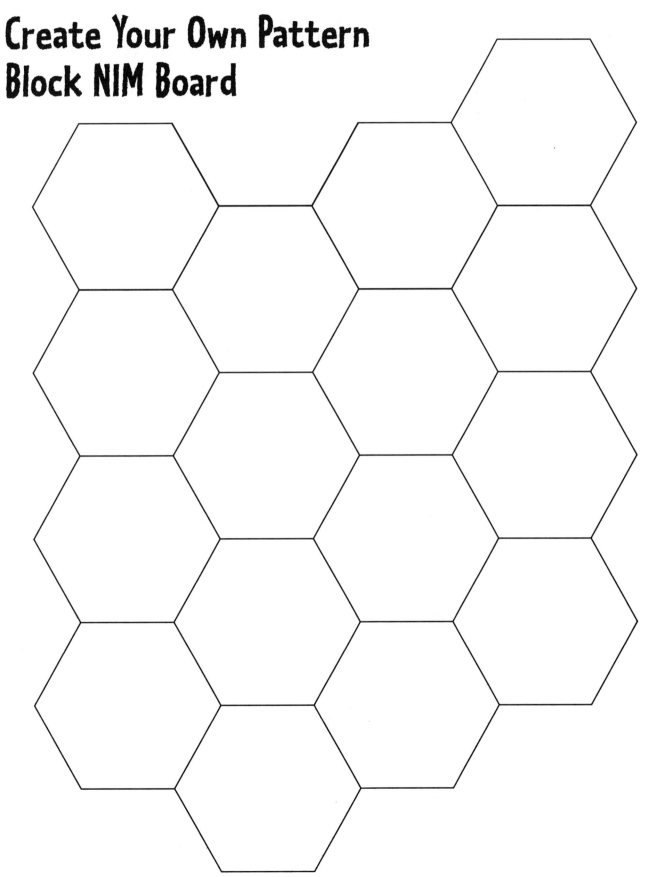

Add-Up NIM

How to Play

1. Choose a target number between 20 and 35. Write this number down.
2. Take turns placing a marker on a number and announcing the sum of all numbers covered to that point. For example, if there are markers already on a 1 and 2, and you place one on a 4 next, you say "seven."
3. Only one marker per square.
4. No skipping turns.
5. The winner places the marker that makes the sum equal to the target number.

4	4	4	4
3	3	3	3
2	2	2	2
1	1	1	1

Add-Up NIM Strategy

Strategy Ideas

What does the range for choosing a target number have to do with the playing board? Does your strategy change as the target number changes? What kinds of patterns can you find? Think about whose turn it will be when there's 5 remaining to reach the target number.

Your Own Strategies

New Game Ideas

- Change the playing boards by adding rows and columns and using different numbers.
- Change the range of target numbers. How does this range relate to the playing board?
- Place markers on the board to equal a selected target number. Take turns removing markers and subtracting from this target until the winner announces "zero."

Your Own Games

Another Add-Up NIM Playing Board

Fraction Add-Up NIM: Select a target number between 1 and 3 that can be reached by adding sixteenths, eighths, fourths, and halves.

$\frac{1}{2}$	$\frac{1}{2}$	$\frac{1}{2}$	$\frac{1}{2}$
$\frac{1}{4}$	$\frac{1}{4}$	$\frac{1}{4}$	$\frac{1}{4}$
$\frac{1}{8}$	$\frac{1}{8}$	$\frac{1}{8}$	$\frac{1}{8}$
$\frac{1}{16}$	$\frac{1}{16}$	$\frac{1}{16}$	$\frac{1}{16}$

Another Add-Up NIM Playing Board

Decimal Add-Up NIM: Select a target number between 1 and 3.5 that can be reached by adding the numbers in the squares.

0.4	0.4	0.4	0.4
0.3	0.3	0.3	0.3
0.2	0.2	0.2	0.2
0.1	0.1	0.1	0.1

Another Add-Up NIM Playing Board

For this version of Fraction Add-Up NIM, select a target number between 1 and 4 that can be reached by adding twelfths, sixths, and thirds.

$\frac{1}{2}$	$\frac{1}{2}$	$\frac{1}{2}$	$\frac{1}{2}$
$\frac{1}{3}$	$\frac{1}{3}$	$\frac{1}{3}$	$\frac{1}{3}$
$\frac{1}{6}$	$\frac{1}{6}$	$\frac{1}{6}$	$\frac{1}{6}$
$\frac{1}{12}$	$\frac{1}{12}$	$\frac{1}{12}$	$\frac{1}{12}$

Triangular NIM

How to Play

1. Place the 12 markers on the triangles of the playing board.
2. Take turns removing 1 or 2 markers at a time.
3. When removing 2 markers, they must be from adjacent triangles.
4. No skipping turns.
5. The winner takes the last 1 or 2 markers.

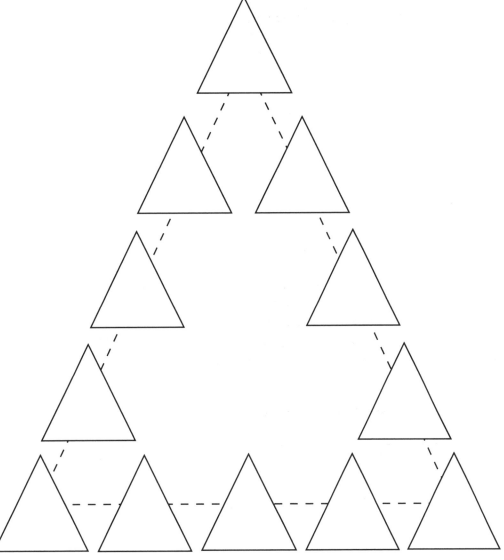

Adjacent triangles are connected by a dotted line.

Triangular NIM Strategy

Strategy Ideas

Make a smaller version of the problem. What if there were 3 triangles? Look for patterns. Try leaving "holes" to isolate markers.

Try the other playing boards on the next page. Can you find a general strategy for boards with an even number of triangles? What about boards with an odd number of triangles? Does this have anything to do with winning strategies?

Your Own Strategies

New Game Ideas

- Change the playing board by adding or subtracting triangles.
- To win, force your opponent to take the last marker.
- Take turns removing up to 3 markers from adjacent triangles.
- Eliminate the adjacent rule. When picking up 2 markers, they can come from anywhere on the board.

Your Own Games

More Triangular
NIM Playing Boards

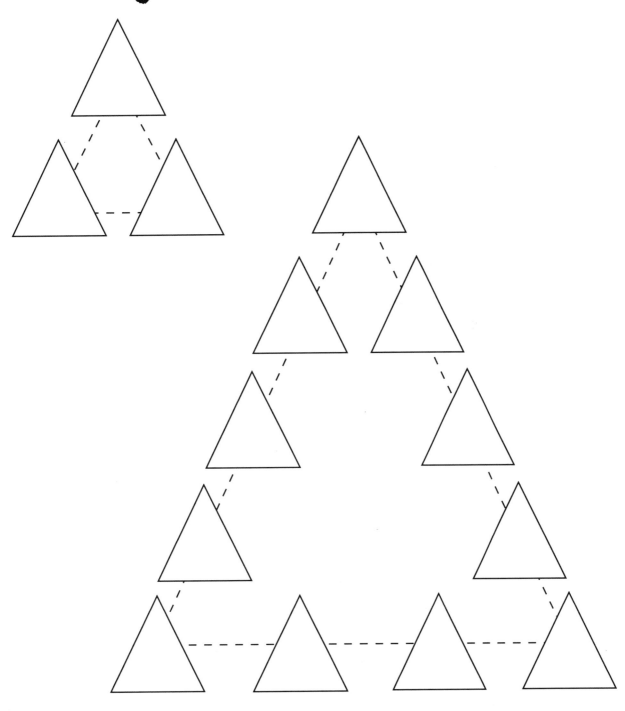

More Triangular
NIM Playing Boards

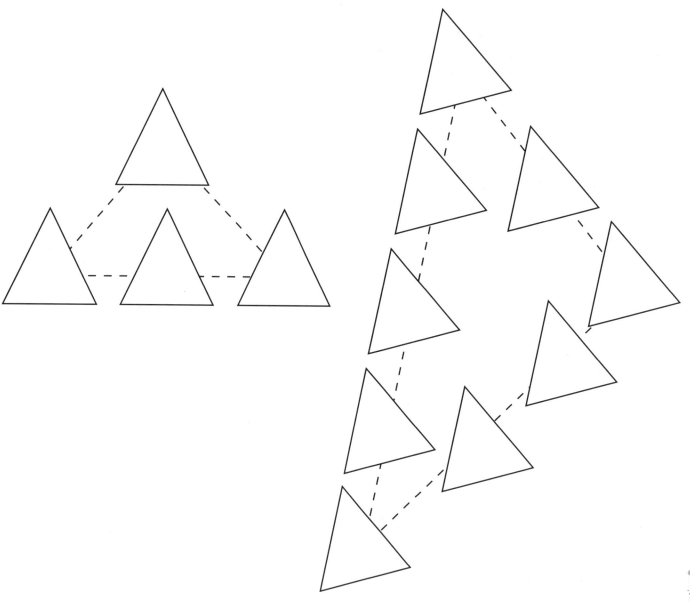

Integer NIM

How to Play

1. One color marker (such as blue) represents a +1. Another color marker (such as white) represents a −1. Combining one of each creates a "powerful zero."
2. Place 5 powerful zeros on the playing area (for example, 5 blue and 5 white).
3. Take turns removing either −2, −1, a powerful zero, +1, or +2. In other worlds, remove 1 or 2 markers in any combination.
4. No skipping turns.
5. The winner removes the last one or two markers and announces the total value of the pieces they have and the total value of their opponent's pieces.

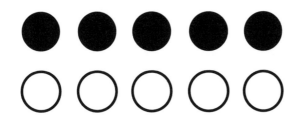

Integer NIM Strategy

Strategy Ideas

Start with a smaller version, such as 2 powerful zeros. Look for patterns.

Your Own Strategies

New Game Ideas

- Change the number of powerful zeros.
- Change what can be taken on a turn.
- Change the definition of winning.

Your Own Games

Path NIM

How to Play

1. If you are the first player, place the marker in one of the squares along the top row.
2. If you are the second player, move the same marker one square to the right, left, or straight down.
3. Take turns moving the marker one square at a time according to the following rules.
4. Do not move the marker up or diagonally.
5. Do not move the marker to a previously occupied square. In other words, a square can be occupied only once during a game. (It helps to mark the used squares with a pencil.)
6. No skipping turns.
7. The winner moves the marker into the goal area.

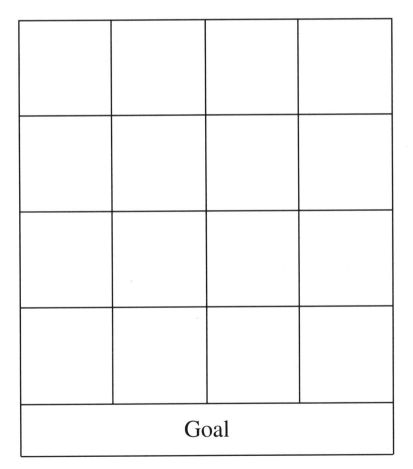

Goal

Path NIM Strategy Ideas

Strategy Ideas

Try the game with a 2-by-2 square grid above the goal. Does the first or second player win? What happens with a 3-by-2 or a 2-by-3 board? After each play, look at the playable squares remaining. How does each move change the dimensions of the playing board?

Your Own Strategies

This game is more complicated than the others in this book. Is it a game of NIM? How would you justify your answer?

New Game Ideas

- Change the playing board.
- To win, force your opponent to move the marker into the goal area.
- Allow diagonal moves.

Your Own Games

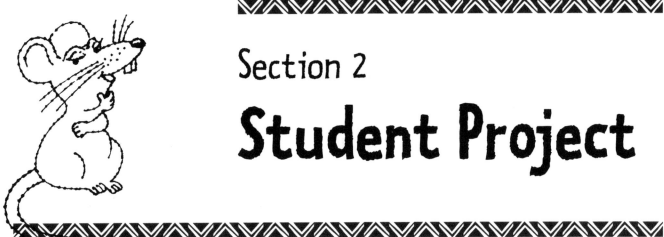

Section 2
Student Project

Project Introduction   43

Student Sheet 1—Project Overview   47

Student Sheet 2—Reminder Page   48

Student Sheet 3—Title and Theme   49

Student Sheet 4—Game Rules   50

Student Sheet 5—Playing Board and Pieces   51

Student Sheet 6—Finishing and Packaging   52

Student Sheet 7—Oral Presentation   53

Student Sheet 8—Evaluation   54

Sample Student Projects and Evaluations   55

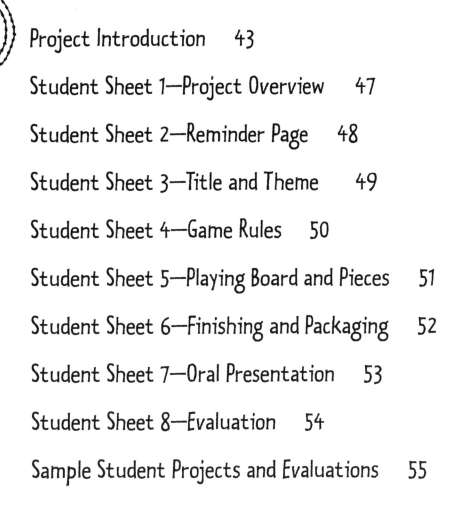

Project Introduction

After students have had ample experience with a variety of NIM games, they are ready to create their own. You must be sure that your students can differentiate between NIM and other types of games. Otherwise, you will likely receive a lot of games of chance, and even some very complicated games that are versions of *Dungeons and Dragons.* Lead a discussion about the essence of NIM (see Student Sheet 1, page 47) or assess students' understanding using the Sprouts game. Do their arguments for and against sprouts being a NIM game show they really understand NIM?

Grouping Students. Give students a choice of working alone or with a partner. By offering students this choice, you accommodate their learning and working styles. Emphasize that they must stick with their decisions until the project is completed.

Sometimes one partner does all the work while the other contributes little. Ask your students to identify strategies for dealing with this problem. Ask, "What can you do to encourage your partner to contribute?" Record students' ideas on chart paper to be posted on the wall. It will be students' responsibility, not yours, to work out any problems related to work distribution and completion during the project.

With your students, review Student Sheet 1—Project Overview and Student Sheet 2—Reminder Page. These summarize what is expected and how evaluation will be handled. Tell students their projects will be submitted in stages to encourage continued work and pacing. The outline here helps you coach students as they work through the process, making the experience more valuable and the final product one of quality.

Assign due dates for each stage of the project to help students pace themselves. To complete the project in four to five weeks, assign about one student sheet per week. Set aside a little class time for project work, but explain that this project is predominantly a homework assignment.

Depending upon the number of projects you will be evaluating, you may want to stagger due dates. For example, have several projects due on Monday, several more on Tuesday, and so on. This way, you can avoid being overwhelmed by a large stack of projects to evaluate all at once.

The final two stages of finishing the game packaging and presenting it orally will consume more time than the first three stages. You might want to schedule specific due dates for each oral presentation, having several a day until everyone has presented.

Student Sheets 3 through 5 include space for providing feedback. Under Comments, check one of the two boxes—either "Sounds fine; you are ready to proceed to the next step," or "Try the following suggestions for improving your game." When you check the second box, write specific suggestions for improving the project. Whether or not you ask students to check with you after making these revisions is up to you.

Title and Theme. Encourage students to choose broad themes. This allows for greater flexibility while developing the game and solving problems as they arise. You might also want to discuss some literary patterns they can use when creating titles. Some helpful patterns include alliteration, rhyming, well-known pairs (knife and fork), portmanteaus (beefalo = beef + buffalo), metaphor, and simile.

Game Rules. Writing rules is problematic for many students. Emphasize that simple statements are the most effective. Take time to reread the rules for the games students have already played. With the class develop a set of rules for a sample NIM game. You could model each stage of the project with a class example (such as Pigs on Parade from Student Sheet 3). The class picks a title and theme, sketches a playing board, plans the playing pieces, writes rules, and so on.

Playing Board and Pieces. Some NIM games, such as calculator NIM and Classic NIM, do not require a playing board. Students need to decide whether or not their games will include boards. For those students making boards, emphasize the importance of space and appropriate sizing. For example, any playing board for Pattern Block NIM must have hexagon spaces the same size as the hexagons in the set of pattern blocks. If a board is going to be covered with 1-inch cubes, the spaces need to be at least 1-inch squares.

As an introduction to creating playing boards, discuss design elements. Show students how to create neat and inviting products by using rulers and templates. Demonstrate how to use templates, rub-on letters, cut-out letters, bubble letters, dot letters, rubber stamps, and so on. Letters either need to be consistently sized or obviously and intentionally distorted. Some students may want to use a word processor.

Consider inviting an artist to bring samples and talk about design—line, shape, form, color, pattern, sizing, and relationships between visual elements.

Discuss materials appropriate for playing boards. Card stock or manila folders work well. Students may choose to write the final drafts of their rules on the playing boards.

The playing pieces should be easy to use and should fit the spaces of the playing board. Brainstorm with students to list some appropriate playing pieces and some that might not work as well. For example, gummy bears are not appropriate—they are sticky, are not long-lasting, and present health problems.

Finishing and Packaging. Encourage students to revise their boards, pieces, and rules until they have a quality product. You may want to provide resealable plastic bags, pocket folders, or boxes for packaging. Or, let students come up with their own packaging. Discuss other packaging considerations. For example, some students may write the rules in more than one language. Others may design a smaller game to save cardboard.

Oral Presentation. Pose the question, "What makes a good oral presentation?" Have students write responses on Student Sheet 7— Oral Presentation. They will use these suggestions as they plan their presentations. You may want to give a time limit, perhaps five minutes for each presentation.

Evaluation. Generally, evaluation scores on the final products should be high. Both you and your students have invested a lot of energy. The points listed on Student Sheet 8 are general and flexible guides. Ask students to help define these areas more specifically. Ask, "What needs to be part of a project in order to get the maximum number of points in each area?" "What might reduce the number of points in each area?" Your students will probably require more than you would. An important aspect of assessment is having students assess themselves and each other. Here are three ideas for completing the evaluations:

1. Make several extra copies of Student Sheet 8—Evaluation for each student. Have each student (or pair, for those that had partners) exchange projects with another student (or pair). They begin by hearing each other's oral presentations and assigning scores on a copy of Student Sheet 8. Then they play the games as they complete the evaluation sheet. Have students

exchange projects several times, until you collect a good number of evaluations for each student or pair. How many exchanges students make depends on how much class time you can spare. Calculate the mean, median, or mode of each student's or pair's collection of evaluation final point scores.

2. Divide the class in groups of four to six students. Give each group enough copies of Student Sheet 8 to complete an evaluation for every other group member. Have all students give their oral presentations to the class. As they do, only their group members fill out evaluation sheets, the rest of the class just listens. After the oral presentations, students break into groups to play each other's games and complete the evaluation sheets. This method gives everyone a chance to see what the other students accomplished.

3. If you choose not to have peer evaluations, have students or pairs give you their blank evaluation sheets just before giving their oral presentations. Fill out the sheets as students present their games. As each presentation concludes, discuss it as a class.

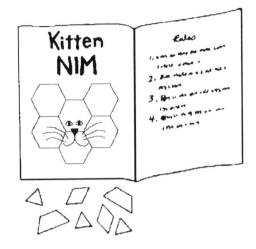

Student Sheet 1 Project Overview

You will be designing an original NIM Game. First think about the essence of NIM games.

- The rules establish a target number or goal. This number can be a collection of things to be placed or removed, such as 10 sticks. This number can also be a goal to reach or a place to begin, such as adding to reach 21 or starting at 21 and subtracting to 0. Or, the target might be determined by the playing board, as in Pattern Block NIM.
- The rules set a range for how many can be played on a turn. For example, you can place (or remove) up to 3 (1, 2, or 3) sticks on a turn. Or, the rule might state that you can place a triangle, a blue rhombus, or a trapezoid pattern block on a turn.
- The rules state how to win the game. For example, you win by taking the last stick or placing the last pattern block. Or, you win by forcing the other player to take (or place) the last stick or pattern block.
- Sometimes there is a special rule describing how things must be placed or removed. For example, if you take 2 sticks, they must be adjacent to each other.
- There is a winning strategy. A true NIM game allows the players to develop a strategy for winning. This might include going first and taking 1 stick; then taking 1 stick if your opponent takes 2 and taking 2 sticks if your opponent takes 1. Each turn is determined by a decision the player makes, not by chance. Games where dice are rolled are games of chance, not NIM games.

You will be asked to submit your plans in stages so you can improve your product based upon recommendations. These are the stages.

1. Think of a title and theme for your game.
2. Write the rules for your game and describe the playing board.
3. Draw the playing board, if this is part of your game, and describe any materials. This description needs to include an explanation of how your board and playing pieces relate to your theme.
4. Package the final version of the game.
5. Give an oral presentation of your game to your classmates.

Student Sheet 2 Reminder Page

Write the due dates for each stage of your project.

Project Stage	Due Date
1. Title and Theme	_____
2. Game Rules	_____
3. Playing Board and Pieces	_____
4. Finishing and Packaging	_____
5. Oral Presentation	_____

Your game will be evaluated on the following 6 items. Keep them in mind as you create your game.

1. Oral presentation was clear and effective. (20 points) _____

2. Game demonstrates an understanding of the essence of NIM. (20 points) _____

3. Rules are clear, easy to read, understandable, and complete. (20 points) _____

4. Complete game package is attractive, neat, inviting, and makes good use

   of design elements such as line, shape, form, color, and pattern. (20 points) _____

5. Game is safe and easy to use. (10 points) _____

6. Game presents an appropriate challenge for the intended audience. (10 points) _____

Total Points (100 possible) _____

7. Bonus points for extra effort, an impressive product, or the effective use of math

   tools such as pattern blocks or Cuisenaire® rods. _____

Final Point Score _____

Name _____

Student Sheet 3 Title and Theme

Think about some of the NIM games you have played. What themes can you identify? For example, in Pattern Block NIM, the game title, playing board, and playing pieces all relate to pattern blocks.

Imagine designing a NIM game around pigs. The title of such a game might be Pigs on Parade. The playing board might show three lines of pigs; the game pieces would be little plastic pigs.

Use this page to record your game title and to specifically describe your theme.

Title
....

Theme Description
....
....
....
....

Comments

❏ Sounds fine; you are ready to proceed to the next step.

❏ Try the following suggestions for improving your game.

Student Sheet 4 Game Rules

Reread Student Sheet 1 about the essence of NIM games. Be sure your rules include a statement for each aspect of NIM. Write your rules in simple terms so they are easy to read and to understand.

Rules
1. Setup (include number of playing pieces and where to put them)
2. Target or Goal
3. How to Play the Pieces
4. How to Win
5. Special Rule (optional)

Hand in a rough-draft sketch of your playing board (if you are using one).

Comments
❑ Sounds fine; you are ready to proceed to the next step.
❑ Try the following suggestions for improving your game.

Student Sheet 5 Playing Board and Pieces

How will you use the playing board (if you plan to use one) and the playing pieces to develop your theme? If your theme is apples, can you make the spaces on your board in the shape of apples? Can you make cardboard apples or find small plastic apples to use as playing pieces? Using real apple seeds as playing pieces is a creative idea, but they would be hard to pick up!

You could add a short story line on the board about Johnny Appleseed, and perhaps depict Johnny's stops along his trek to plant apple trees. Or, perhaps your playing board will be an apple orchard. Players take turns picking apples from the trees. Be creative!

Design your playing board, then draw it on an $8\frac{1}{2}$-by-11-inch piece of paper. Make it very neat. Make the spaces on your board the right size for the playing pieces. Draw straight lines using a ruler, unless you want to make neat wavy lines. Make your lettering either perfectly straight or intentionally staggered or bubbled. You may want to include your rules on your playing board. Attach your playing board to this sheet with a paper clip. Describe your playing pieces in detail below.

Description of Playing Pieces

Comments

❑ Sounds fine; you are ready to proceed to the next step.

❑ Try the following suggestions for improving your game.

Student Sheet 6 — Finishing and Packaging

Think about games you have purchased or received as gifts. What makes them inviting to play? How are they packaged? You need to package your rules, playing pieces, and board in a durable, neat, and inviting way. Here are some areas to consider as you finish and package your game.

Playing Board

- Is it neat, attractive, and inviting?
- Is it sized appropriately? Do the playing pieces fit on the board spaces?
- Is it sturdy and durable?

Playing Pieces

- Are they neat, attractive, and inviting?
- Are they sized appropriately? Do they fit on the playing board? Are they easy to handle and store?
- Are they safe to use?
- Are they durable?

Rules

- Are they easy to read and understand?
- Are they printed or typed neatly?

Packaging

- Is it neat, attractive, and inviting?
- It is easy to repackage the game? Does it store conveniently?
- Is it durable and sturdy?
- Is it recyclable?

Game

- Is it inviting to a variety of groups when considering age, gender, and culture?
- Is it challenging?
- Is it free of violence?

Make a final version of your rules, playing board, and playing pieces, and then package it as a final product.

Student Sheet 7 Oral Presentation

Think about what makes a good oral presentation. Consider these suggestions.

- Make eye contact with the audience.
- Speak loudly and clearly.
- Be organized. Have all materials and visuals ready.
- Actively involve the audience.
- Involve your partner in the presentation (if you have one).
- Use appropriate pacing. Don't go too fast or too slow.

Use this page to outline your presentation.

Name ....

Student Sheet 8 Evaluation

Use the space under each item to write a minimum of one positive comment. This could include something about the quality of the project or a positive suggestion for improvement.

Evaluation for _____
                    Name(s)

1. Oral presentation was clear and effective. (20 points)

2. Game demonstrates an understanding of the essence of NIM. (20 points)

3. Rules are clear, easy to read, understandable, and complete. (20 points)

4. Complete game package is attractive, neat, inviting, and makes good use

   of design elements such as line, shape, form, color, and pattern. (20 points)

5. Game is safe and easy to use. (10 points)

6. Game presents an appropriate challenge for the intended audience. (10 points)

                                    Total Points (100 possible) _____

7. Bonus points for extra effort, an impressive product, or effective use of math tools.

                                          Final Point Score _____

Sample Student Projects and Evaluations

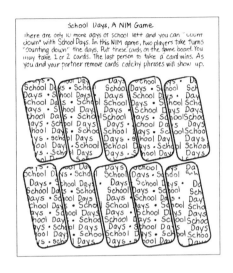

School Days

Students can create games similar to any of the NIM games. "School Days" (page 60 to 61) is an example of a game organized into an array.

The theme was timely as the project was assigned toward the end of the school year. Sara's playing board and pieces carry out the theme effectively. The rules are easy to read and understand and show evidence of understanding the essence of NIM. The rhymes on the playing board demonstrate creativity.

I'm concerned that the student replicated the "Balloon Ride" version of NIM. Even though her playing board is an array, she has not used the arrangement in the rules. I would recommend that she revise her rules to include spatial limitations. For example, if a player takes two cards on one turn, they must be from adjacent cells, those sharing a side and not just a corner. I would also suggest that the student use a real calendar as a basis for arranging these last ten days. She might conduct some research and determine the dates and days of the week of the last ten days of school. If she did this for the past six or seven years, her lifetime in school, she could create as many as seven different playing boards.

The student also needs to work on packaging her game. Her board and playing pieces are made on regular paper. I would recommend placing the board in a sheet protector or recreating it and the playing pieces with card stock. She could also improve the appearance of the game by adding some color and more illustrations on the board. As it stands, I would give this project these points.

1. Oral presentation — 20 of 20 points
2. Essence of NIM — 20 of 20 points
3. Rules — 20 of 20 points
4. Packaging — 13 of 20 points
5. Safe and easy to use — 8 of 10 points
6. Appropriate challenge — 3 of 10 points
7. no extra points

Final Score: 84 of 100 points

By following the recommendations, the student might raise her score to over 100 points with extra points for research into the dates and calendar arrangements of the last ten days of school over the past seven years.

M&M MMaddness!

This game (page 62) is an example of games designed with a path. Food and sports are both popular themes for this style NIM game. This student has carried out his theme in the board and playing pieces. The hands on the board are a nice reference to how "m&m's® melt in your mouth, not in your hands." The title shows creativity with spelling to include the double *m*'s.

I'm concerned that the rules do not make it clear that players must start at the beginning and put pieces in order along the path to the end at the guy's mouth. I'm sure this was the intent, otherwise winning is simple by going first and placing a marker on the guy's mouth.

The playing board is crowded. I would recommend that the student write the rules on a separate rule sheet and remove some of the extra lines. The word *Start* at the beginning of the path would also help. I'd also recommend creating a facsimile of real m&m's® as playing pieces rather than using real candy. As it stands, I would assign these points.

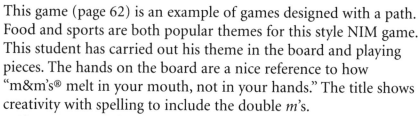

1. Oral presentation   20 of 20 points
2. Essence of NIM   20 of 20 points
3. Rules   10 of 20 points
4. Packaging   13 of 20 points
5. Safe and easy to use   5 of 10 points
6. Appropriate challenge   6 of 10 points
7. no extra points

Final Score: 74 of 100 points

Koala Race

This project (page 63) includes a playing mat for pieces with no special arrangement or order indicated. The playing pieces are markers that cover the leaves on the playing board. The rules are clear. I would comment on the title, "Since there is no path, why did you use *race* in your title?"

The playing board is neat, but with the markers in place, it is very crowded. Also, the board is not sturdy and durable and should be placed in a sheet protector or redone on card stock.

The student might improve the challenge presented by her game by changing the rules so that the players decide together how many leaves to cover prior to beginning play. The student's oral presentation clearly explained the game and gave information about the diet of koala bears. As it stands, I would assign points as follows:

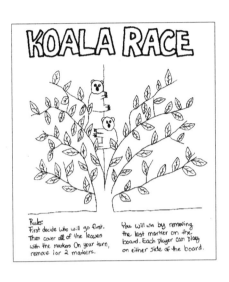

KOALA RACE

Rules:
First decide who will go first. Then cover all of the leaves with the markers On your turn, remove 1 or 2 markers.

You will win by removing the last marker on the board. Each player can play on either side of the board.

1. Oral presentation	20 of 20 points
2. Essence of NIM	20 of 20 points
3. Rules	20 of 20 points
4. Packaging	10 of 20 points
5. Safe and easy to use	7 of 10 points
6. Appropriate challenge	6 of 10 points
7. Extra points for the creative addition to her oral report	2

Final Score: 85 of 100 points

Run Around the Clock

Set the clock for twelve.
Pick any time. Add minutes.
The first person to reach the time wins.

Run Around the Clock

Some students will create something more unusual. Run Around the Clock (page 64) uses the standard clock face as a playing board. This game allows players to establish a target time. They set the clock for 12:00 and then take turns advancing the hands to reach the target. The winner is the person who reaches the target time.

The rules for this game need further definition. Should there be some limits for setting a target time? For example, should these times be multiples of five minutes rather than times such as 2:37? The number of minutes a player can advance on a turn must be established. For example, the rules could specify a player may advance the clock 5, 10, or 15 minutes at a time.

This game could become very challenging with further development. What if one player sets the target time and the second player sets the starting time rather than always beginning at 12:00? What if these times included A.M. and P.M? for example, the target time is 1:00 P.M. and the starting time is 6:00 A.M. This game has the added benefit of involving players in tracking time which is also difficult for some students. The clock could use more color, but it is sturdy and the cardboard hands attached with a round-head fastener move easily. The game was packaged in a ziplock bag. Assuming the oral presentation was good, I would assign these points.

1. Oral presentation	20 of 20 points
2. Essence of NIM	10 of 20 points
3. Rules	5 of 20 points
4. Packaging	12 of 20 points
5. Safe and easy to use	8 of 10 points
6. Appropriate challenge	5 of 10 points
7. no extra points	

Final Score: 60 of 100 points

Recommendations on Student Sheet 4 should help a student make needed changes in the rules before the final project is submitted. If the rules were clarified, the scores on both 2 and 3 would go up.

Tangram Tangle and Transformation

This project (pages 65 to 68) is a good example of how a student has used a math manipulative. Players place *tans*, pieces from tangram sets, on a square playing board that is the same size as the original square from which the tangrams were created. In this case, the square is three inches on a side. Lines have been added to the square that divide the area into 32 small triangles and the tans must be placed so the sides correspond with these lines.

The playing board is neat, inviting, and it includes small figures created from small tangrams. The black and white format is attractive and shows attention to design.

This student put in extra effort by suggesting ways to change and extend the game. The original game is accessible to everyone, and the extensions provide further challenges.

The notes on the product packaging were a nice added touch, and they help players return all the materials appropriately.

As part of his oral report, this students read a story about tangrams and shared information about the origin of tangrams. The student even created figures on the overhead projector while telling the story. I would assign these points

1. Oral presentation	20 of 20 points	
2. Essence of NIM	20 of 20 points	
3. Rules	20 of 20 points	
4. Packaging	20 of 20 points	
5. Safe and easy to use	10 of 10 points	
6. Appropriate challenge	10 of 10 points	
7. Extra points for extensions, packaging notes, creative oral presentation	6	

Final Score: 106 of 100 points

Tangram Tangle

Playing Pieces: 2 sets of traditional tangrams based on a 3-inch square. 14 tans in all.

How to Play:
- Take turns placing 1 tan on the playing board.
- Each piece must be placed so its sides line up with the lines on the playing board.

  OK   NOT OK
- No skipping turns.
- The winner places the last piece possible.

Tangram Tangle
Transformation

When you figure out how to win Tangram Tangle try these variations:
- Use more sets of Tangrams.
- The winner forces the other person to place the last piece.
- Create new playing boards.

  Notice that the original playing board has 32 small triangles... new boards might be a different arrangement of 32 small triangles or have a different number of small triangles. Use the Tangle Transformation grid to cut out your new playing boards.
- Allow placing 1 or 2 tans which must be placed so that they share a side.
- Create new tan pieces... what if one of the...

Tangram Tangle and Transformation
Packaging Information
This Game Pack Contains
- Directions for Tangram Tangle
- Directions for Tangram Tangle Transformation
  these are placed back to back in a sleeve protector with cardstock sandwiched between for "stiffness."
- 8 sets of Tangrams cut from "Craft Foam" each of these is a different color and bagged separately into small plastic bags, resealable.
- 25 copies of Tangram Tangle Transformation Grid these are on regular white bond paper and will need to be replenished as consumed for making new boards.
- 1 pair of scissors

All these are packaged in a jumbo resealable bag with a hole punched in a top corner to help avoid bag popping.

Sample Student Project 1

School Days, A NIM Game

There are only 10 more days of school left and you can "count down" with School Days. In this NIM game, two players take turns "counting down" the days. Put these cards on the game board. You may take 1 or 2 cards. The last person to take a card wins. As you and your partner remove cards catchy phrases will show up.

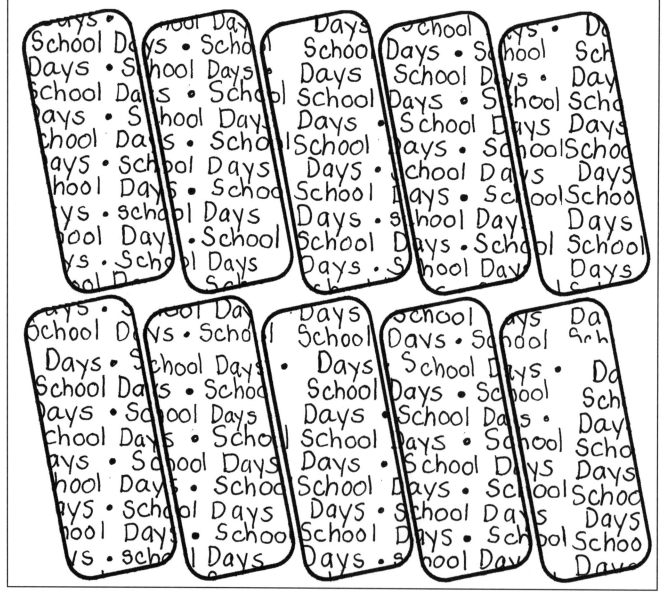

Sample Student Project 1

School Days
A NIM Game

·10·
Play these 10 and you will win.

·9·
When school is out, no more will I pout.

·8·
Party 'till you drop, your Mom won't say STOP!!!

·7·
We get to sleep late – Can you wait?

·6·
Summer's friends are just around the bend.

·5·
To paradise I'm going to get my vacation flowing.

·4·
I'm going to prance at the 6<u>th</u> grade dance.

·3·
Almost there. It's hard to bear.

·2·
After today we can play!

·1·
Yay!! School's Out!

Sample Student Project 3

KOALA RACE

Rules:
First decide who will go first. Then cover all of the leaves with the markers. On your turn, remove 1 or 2 markers.

You will win by removing the last marker on the board. Each player can play on either side of the board.

Run Around the Clock

Set the clock for twelve.
Pick any time. Add minutes.
The first person to reach the time wins.

Tangram Tangle

Playing Pieces: 2 sets of traditional tangrams based on a 3-inch square 14 tans in all

How to Play:

- Take turns placing 1 tan on the playing board.

- Each piece must be placed so its sides line up with the lines on the playing board.

OK   NOT OK

- No skipping turns.

- The winner places the last piece possible.

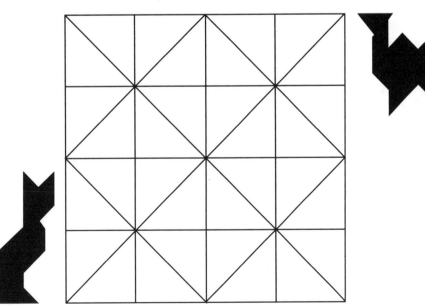

Tangram Tangle
Transformation

When you figure out how to win Tangram Tangle try these variations:

- Use more sets of Tangrams.

- The winner forces the other person to place the last piece.

- Create new playing boards.

  Notice that the original playing board has 32 small triangles... new boards might be a different arrangement of 32 small triangles or have a different number of small triangles.

  Use the Tangle Transformation grid to cut out your new playing boards.

- Allow placing 1 or 2 tans which must be placed so that they share a side.

- Create new tan pieces... what if one of the pieces looked like this:

Sample Student Project 5

Tangram Tangle and Transformation
Packaging Information
This Game Pack Contains

- Directions for Tangram Tangle

- Directions for Tangram Tangle Transformation
  these are placed back to back in a sleeve protector with cardstock sandwiched between for "stiffness."

- 8 sets of Tangrams cut from "Craft Foam"
  each of these is a different color and bagged separately into small plastic bags, resealable.

- 25 copies of Tangram Tangle Transformation Grid
  these are on regular white bond paper and will need to be replenished as consumed for making new boards.

- 1 pair of scissors

All these are packaged in a jumbo reseable bag with a hole punched in a top corner to help avoid bag popping.

Sample Student Project 5

Tangram Tangle and Transformation Grid

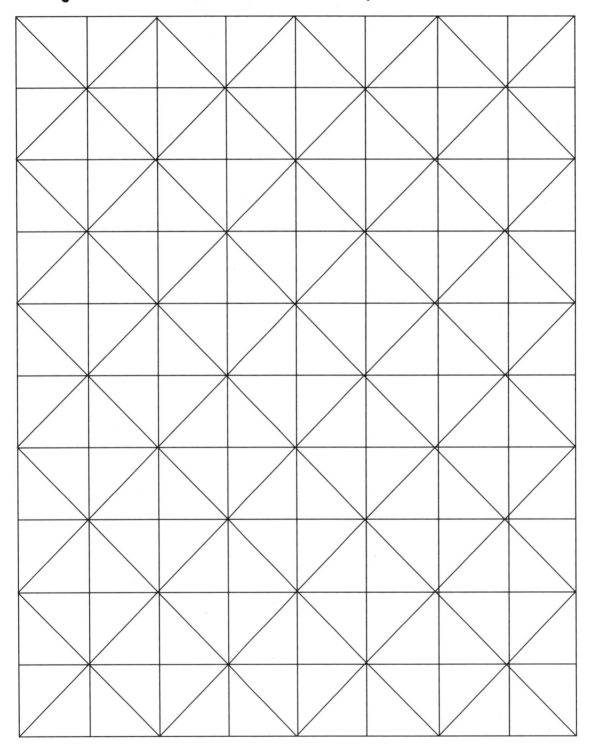